D1563902

The World My Church

Learning and Loving My Orthodox Faith

Fr John Chryssavgis
Sophie Chryssavgis

HOLY CROSS ORTHODOX PRESS
Brookline, Massachusetts

This book is kindly sponsored by
Dr Thomas and Anna Leontis
of Columbus, Ohio

Young children discover and learn to communicate with the world around them through their senses of touch, smell, taste, hearing and sight. This discovery is as important for the child's intellectual development as more abstract concepts will be later on.

The first perception of God, the first sense of what is divine and holy, comes to the young child through the physical senses too. Jesus Christ showed this clearly when He "became indignant" with His disciples who tried to prevent mothers from bringing their babies to Him: He took the children in His arms, blessed them, laid His hands on them. He made them feel His love not by speaking about it, not even by telling them a story, but through bodily contact.

The first experience of church life comes to a young child through seeing and touching church objects, feeling drops of holy water or oil, smelling incense, kissing an icon, tasting Holy Communion. It is only a beginning, a seed, but a truly valid beginning, a truly living seed. A long process of growth and development will be necessary for a child to become a mature Christian, yet this long process begins in the very first years of life. Familiarity with church objects helps a young child to feel at home in the church, and feeling comfortable in familiar surroundings is a first step towards loving the church.

A first step is a first step only. There is a long way to go before a human being reaches the ability to run a race, to climb a mountain, to perform a dance. Effort, help, care and guidance are needed at all stages, but first steps are important and their value is real — as real as any later achievement.

This book should prove a most useful tool in assisting parents to make church objects familiar, interesting and beloved to their little children.

Sophie Koulomzin

The World My Church has been written
for a brave little boy, Alexander,
and, in the radiance of his eyes,
dedicated to all his known and
unknown friends at Paddington.

In My Home

Jesus

Jesus loves all the people
in the world.
Jesus loves your mother and
your father,
and especially you.

Panagia

Panagia is the mother of God.
She loves all the children in the world.
Look! Here she is holding baby Jesus.

prayer

Prayer is talking to Jesus
and Panagia.
See these children praying?
Do you know how to pray?

Our Father

Our Father
who art in heaven,
hallowed be Thy name;
Thy kingdom come;
Thy will be done,
on earth as it is in heaven.
Give us this day our
daily bread.
And forgive us
our trespasses as we forgive
those who trespass against
us. And lead us not
into temptation,
but deliver us from evil.

Πάτερ ἡμῶν

Πάτερ ἡμῶν
ὁ ἐν τοῖς οὐρανοῖς,
ἁγιασθήτω τὸ ὄνομά σου·
ἐλθέτω ἡ Βασιλεία σου·
γεννηθήτω τὸ θέλημά σου,
ὡς ἐν οὐρανῷ
καὶ ἐπὶ τῆς γῆς.
Τὸν ἄρτον ἡμῶν τὸν
ἐπιούσιον δὸς ἡμῖν σήμερον.
Καὶ ἄφες ἡμῖν
τὰ ὀφειλήματα ἡμῶν,
ὡς καὶ ἡμεῖς ἀφίεμεν
τοῖς ὀφειλέταις ἡμῶν.
Καὶ μὴ εἰσενέγκῃς ἡμᾶς εἰς
πειρασμόν,
ἀλλὰ ῥῦσαι ἡμᾶς ἀπὸ τοῦ
πονηροῦ . . .

cross

You cross yourself
to remember Jesus
and Panagia.
You can cross yourself
before you eat,
to thank them for your food;
before you sleep, to thank
them for your day.

oil lamp

The oil lamp is in front of
Jesus and Panagia.
Do you have an oil lamp at
home?
You can watch your mother
and father light it.

hand censer

With the hand censer
you bless the whole house —
your room, your bed,
your toys.

priest

The priest is a person who
teaches us about
Jesus and Panagia.
When you see him,
kiss his hand
and he will bless you.

In the House
of God

going to church

Can you see the church with
the cross?
It is the house of God.
People come together to
church to pray and sing
to Jesus and Panagia.

candle

As you enter the church,
you can light a candle.
It is a way of showing that
you want Jesus to shine
inside you.

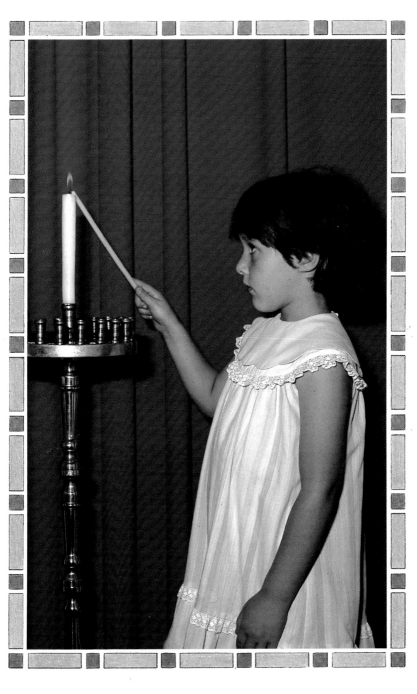

censer

In the church, the priest
holds the censer
and blesses Jesus, Panagia,
you and all the people.

holy communion

In the church, the priest
gives you holy communion.
It is the body and blood of
Jesus. When you take
holy communion,
Jesus comes to be with you
and stays with you.

antidoro

After holy communion,
the priest gives you
a piece of bread which has
been blessed.
This bread is brought by
the people for everyone
to share.

baptism

On the day of baptism,
a child is brought to church
and receives its name
as a christian.
The child is dipped in water
by the priest and
blessed by God.

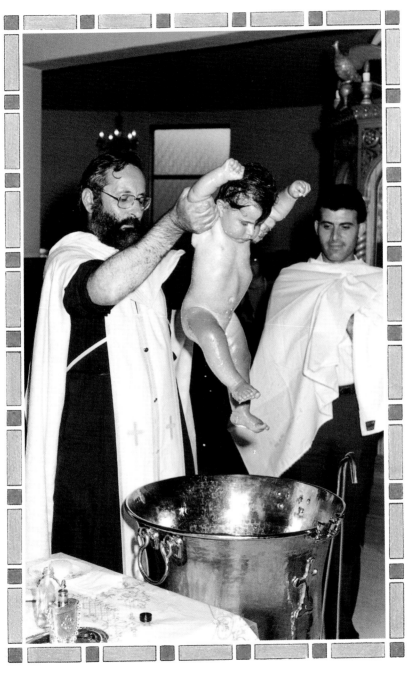

My baptism

I was baptised at

Saint Basil's church

on

_____

I received the name

Kalli

My godparent is

_____

The priest was

_____

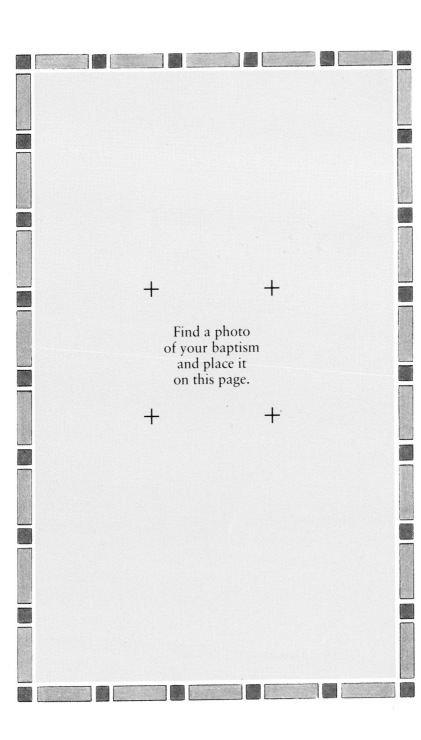

Find a photo
of your baptism
and place it
on this page.

angel

Each one of us has our own
guardian angel,
sent by God to be with us.
Your guardian angel always
takes care of you.

Ὁ ΦΥΛΑΞ ἈΓΓΕΛΟΣ

GUARDIAN ANGEL

...TAKE ME BY MY WRETCHED AND OUTSTRETCHED HAND

Heaven on Earth

Easter

Christ is risen!
Χριστός ἀνέστη!
Easter is the day when Jesus
rose from the dead.
It is the greatest feast of our
church.

Christmas

Christmas is the birthday of Jesus.
Can you see baby Jesus with his mother?
What else do you see?
Christmas is celebrated on the 25th of December.

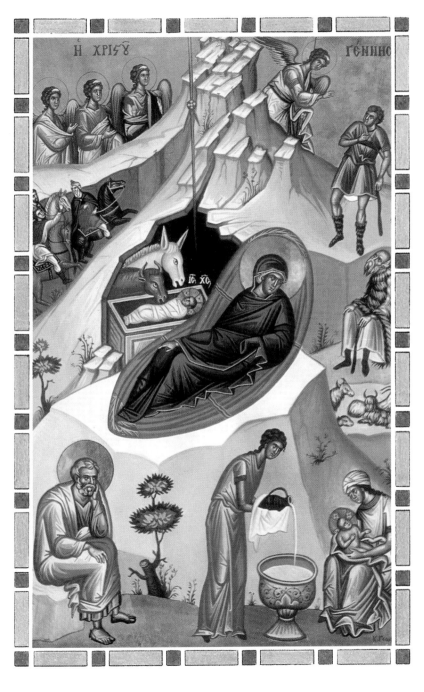

Epiphany

Epiphany is the day Jesus was baptised.
On this day, the priest blesses with holy water the people, their houses and the waters.
Can you see St John baptising Jesus?
Epiphany is celebrated on the 6th of January.

Η ΒΑ   ΠΤΙСΙС

Saint George

Saint George was a young
soldier who protected
and took care of people.
What can you see in the
icon?
His feast day is on the 23rd
of April.

Saint Sophia

Saint Sophia was the mother
of three girls,
whose names were Faith,
Hope and Love. They lived
a very long time ago.
In our church, little children
too are saints.
Their feast day is on the
17th of September.

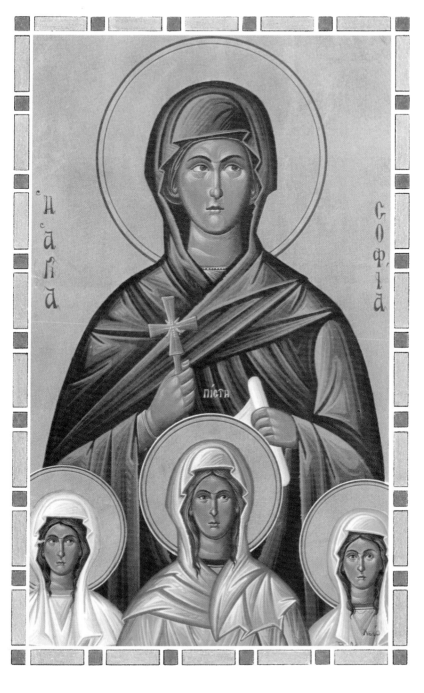

Saint Nektarios

Saint Nektarios was a
bishop. He lived
at a monastery in Greece,
not very long ago.
Saint Nektarios healed many
sick people with his prayers.
He also taught young people
about God.
His feast day is on the 9th of
November.

Ὁ ΑΓΙΟΣ   ΝΕΚΤΑΡΙΟΣ
ὁ ΑΙΓΙΝΗΣ

My name day

My name is

Kalli

My saint is

My name day is on

How do you celebrate your name day?

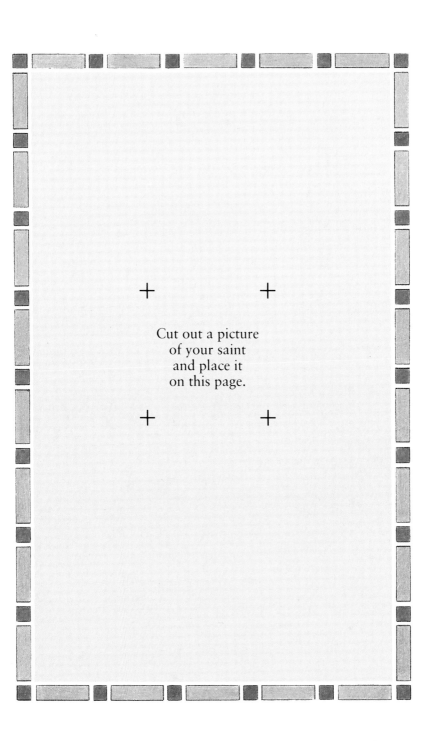

+ +

Cut out a picture
of your saint
and place it
on this page.

+ +

Revised 1998
Originally published in 1990
© Copyright, 1998 Holy Cross Orthodox Press
Published by Holy Cross Orthodox Press
50 Goddard Avenue
Brookline, Massachusetts 02445
USA

ISBN 0-917651-80-4

Acknowledgments:

Photographs
Front cover: Andrew Chryssavgis
Back cover: Courtesy Greek National Tourist Organization
Dr. Steve Zantiotis: pp. 11, 15, 17, 19, 27, 29
Andrew Chryssavgis: pp. 21, 25, 31, 33
Icons: Stavronikita Monastery
Astir Publications (K. Georgakopoulos)
Holy Transfiguration Monastery, Brookline
Apergi Publications
V. Lepouras
Rev. J. Kallis
M. Antoniou